BATH A

Text by Bernard St

Contents

Visitors' Guide	opposite
Rector's Welcome	2
History Chart	3
The Saxon Church	4
The Norman Cathedral	6
Bishop Oliver King	8
The Nave 1750 and Today	10
The Lantern of the West	12
Georgian Elegance – Victorian Revival	14
The Monuments	16
Bells, Books and Candlesticks	18

Left: (15)
The processional cross – a hand wrought, chiselled and repoussé silver cross by Omar Ramsden. The obverse shows *The Adoration of the Shepherds*; the reverse displays *The Adoration of the Kings*.

Rector's Welcome

In offering you this guide to Bath Abbey, we hope that your visit will be enhanced by a clearer understanding of the building and of its history; but, of course, it is impossible to appreciate a church building at the deepest level without looking at the purpose for which it was built and which it serves today.

Bath Abbey exists for the worship of God and to house a large and lively congregation. It is because we believe that God comes to us uniquely in Jesus, to open up for us a new life, that we gather here week by week to praise him, and go out from here to serve him.

Bath Abbey has been called 'The Lantern of the West', and we are currently engaged in polishing that lantern. Our six-project programme, Bath Abbey 2000, aims to conserve the west front; re-light the Abbey; construct an underground display of our history (the Heritage Vaults); clean the interior; rebuild the organ; and clean the rest of the exterior. The total cost of this programme will be £2.5 million.

We aim to complete this work before our Quincentenary in 1999. If you would like to help us in this task, your gift should be sent to Bath Abbey Trust, 13 Kingston Buildings, Bath BA1 1LT. Your help will be most gratefully acknowledged.

At the end of the day, however, it is in the congregation and not just in the building that the light must shine. It is Christ, the light of the world, who illuminates our lives. May his light guide you and give you joy.

Richard Askew

History Chart

Up to the 5th century
Roman occupation of Bath. Pagan temples. Some evidence of individual conversions to Christianity.

577 Battles of Dyrham, Gloucester and Cirencester. Saxon conquest of Bath.

676 Abbess Bertana established by King Osric.

757 Grant of land to monastic brothers of St Peter.

781 Mercian King Offa takes control of monastery.

973 Edgar crowned King of England in Bath Abbey.

1013 Danish (Viking) attacks.

1088 Sack of Bath – rebellion and conflict among barons. Bishop John de Villula consecrated Bishop of Wells.

1090 Transfer of cathedral status from Wells to Bath.

1107 New cathedral building started in Bath.

1192 Bishop Savaric elected Bishop of Bath and Glastonbury.

1244 Roger of Salisbury elected 1st Bishop of Bath and Wells.

1499 Bishop Oliver King commences building new church.

1515 Prior Birde Chantry built.

1539 Dissolution of monasteries by Henry VIII.

1574 Queen Elizabeth I visits – orders completion of the church's restoration.

1608 Bishop Montagu roofs the nave.

1836 Simeon Trust buys advowson from Bath Corporation.

1860 Major restoration by Sir George Gilbert Scott.

1942 Bath bombed during war. East window destroyed.

1960 Post-war restoration completed.

1973 Queen Elizabeth II visits to commemorate *Monarchy 1,000* year.

1991 Major conservation programme commences.

The Saxon Church

Those of us who have the privilege of regular worship in this church know that within these walls we are, in the words of the Prayer Book, 'gathered together in the presence of Almighty God and the whole company of Heaven'. Visitors of many races and origins recognize this as a holy place: the grace and harmony of design seem to make this a tangible emotion.

This is probably the third church to stand on this site. A glance at the history chart on the previous page reminds us that there is evidence of the conversion of some Romans here to the Christian faith. Later, Pope Gregory the Great put into effect his design for a Roman mission and appointed Augustine to spread the faith across England. Augustine passed through Bath in AD 603, and by 676 the monastery at 'Hat Bathu' received its first royal endowment from Osric, King of the Hwicce (a sub-kingdom of Mercia), when Abbess Bertana founded a house of nuns. By 757, a grant of land from King Offa of Mercia was made to the 'brethren in the Monastery of St Peter at Bath'. Contemporary chronicles speak of the wonderful workmanship of the Saxon abbey. The building of this early church must have been influenced by the store of shaped stones in the nearby ruins of the Roman temple, which provided a ready supply of building material. Although we still lack archaeological evidence, it can be assumed that the Saxon church stood on, or close to, the present site.

Within two centuries of its foundation the Saxon abbey had become one of the foremost churches in England and continued to enjoy royal patronage. Bath was also an important river crossing and frontier post between Mercia and Wessex. These factors led to the choice of this church for the coronation of King Edgar on Whit Sunday, 11 May 973, by Dunstan, Archbishop of Canterbury and Oswald, Archbishop of York. The order of service and the symbols of royalty employed on that occasion have been a strong influence on coronation ceremonies up to this day.

There is evidence that the Saxon abbey suffered greatly in the Danish attacks on Bath in 1013.

The Coronation of King Edgar

'Mickle Bliss' says the Saxon Chronicle 'was enjoyed at Bath on that happy day' when 'a crowd of priests and throng of monks, in counsel sage, were gathered there'.

Right:
King Edgar portrayed on the foundation charter of New Minster, Winchester, dated 966. This picture illustrates the close connection between royal authority and the great monastic reform movement. King Edgar (959-75) established a peaceful rule after 50 years of complex warfare, and his coronation, late in his reign, established a new era of peace and the rule of law.

Top left:
The Edgar window. This memorial to Herbert Brice Mundy (1869-1943) was installed in 1949, and depicts the coronation ceremony which began the long line of the English monarchy. Queen Elizabeth II and Prince Philip came to Bath Abbey for the commemorative service in 1973 to celebrate 1,000 years of monarchy, and a tablet to recall their visit may be found on the floor close to the lectern.

Left:
St Aldhelm's cross. This arm of an 8th-century Wessex cross was found near the Cross Bath. It is said that it was originally set up to mark the resting place of the saint's body when it was being carried from a church in the Mendips to Malmesbury for burial.

The Norman Cathedral

The conquest of England by William and the Norman knights in the 11th century led to a period of great unrest as they gradually took control of the country – a period of revolt and rebellion and a time of vigorous and bloody opposition to the new rulers.

On the death of William the Conqueror in 1087, the ownership of Bath and its abbey passed to William Rufus. But the wealthy barons, including Bishop Geoffrey of Coutances whose barony comprised one-tenth of Somerset, rose against the king, singled out the royal borough of Bath and destroyed it in 1088.

John de Villula, a native of Tours, chaplain and physician to the king, was consecrated Bishop of Wells by Archbishop Lanfranc at Canterbury in July 1088. As a reward for personal service, Rufus granted him 'the Abbey of St Peter with all its possessions belonging thereto, that he may set up his chair'. For a sum of 'five hundred pounds of silver' the bishop bought from the king the ruined city with its thermal springs, its mint, royal rights and property. With his Norman fraternity of trained architects and builders, Bishop John aspired to raise the borough to an eminence befitting the dignity of an episcopal see. Before the turn of the century, work commenced on a church some 354 feet (108m) in length by 72 feet (22m) in width. It was very large: the present abbey occupies only the space of the Norman nave. The solidity of masonry can still be gauged from sections of column bases below the floor of the present abbey. Much of the building remained unfinished at the death of the bishop in 1122.

To the south of the cathedral, Bishop John de Villula planned his episcopal buildings, consisting of his palace, cloisters and chapter house; also a guest house and prior's lodgings which held a large communal hall or 'great chamber'.

> *This John de Villula pullid down the old Chirch of St Peter at Bath (the Church of Offa) and erected a new, much fairer, and was buried in the middle of the Presbyterie thereof, whose Image I saw lying there, an 9 Yere sins, at the which tyme the Chirch that he made lay to wast and was unrofid, and redes grew about this John of Tours Sepulchre.'*
> JOHN LELAND'S ITINERARY: PUBLISHED 1549

The baths remained under the control of the church for a further 450 years.

Being a man of culture, Villula established a collegiate school where Adelard of Bath received his early education. Through this medieval scholar, the elements of mathematics and science were brought from the east and introduced into western scholarship.

Bath owed much to the priory for its prosperity. Pilgrimages to the healing centre increased, and hospitals for the amelioration of disease and destitution were inaugurated in the 12th century.

Right:
The Norman Chapel. Around the memorial window is an arch of the 12th-century Norman cathedral, which gave access from the south aisle to the south transept. It has roll-mouldings and is supported by a column with block capital and a chamfered abacus.

and the body of the church paved.

We have to thank Sir John Harington (godson of Queen Elizabeth) for obtaining the necessary £1,000 from the bishop for this work. It is related that they were walking together and were caught in a violent rain storm. Sir John invited the bishop to shelter in the church, and as they stood in the roofless nave, the prelate complained it was just as wet. This provided Sir John with the opportunity for his well-known remark, 'If it keep not us safe from the waters above, how shall it ever save others from the fire beneath?'

It will be noted from the 1750 illustration of the nave on page 10 that the ceiling provided by Bishop Montagu was of decorated plasterwork. A screen divided the choir from the nave, which itself is unfurnished by any seating, apart from the bench round the outer walls, for the old and infirm, where 'the weakest go to the wall'.

During the Civil War the abbey escaped serious damage, although Cromwell's troops were for a time billeted within the church. 'That fayre, neat and lightsome building with large windows' soon became widely known as the 'Lantern of the West'.

> Letter from Sir John Harington, Greenwich,
> 13 June 1608
>
> *'Onlie my old friend, you may not forgett to be a benefactor to BATH CHURCH in your lifetime; for Alms in one's life is like a light borne before one, whereas Alms after death is like a candle carried behind ... Whensoever you will go to Bathe, the Baths would strengthen your sinews; the Alms would strengthen your soule ...'*
>
> and in a further fund-raising effort later the same year:
>
> *'In doing good use no delay
> For tyme ys swift and slydes away'*

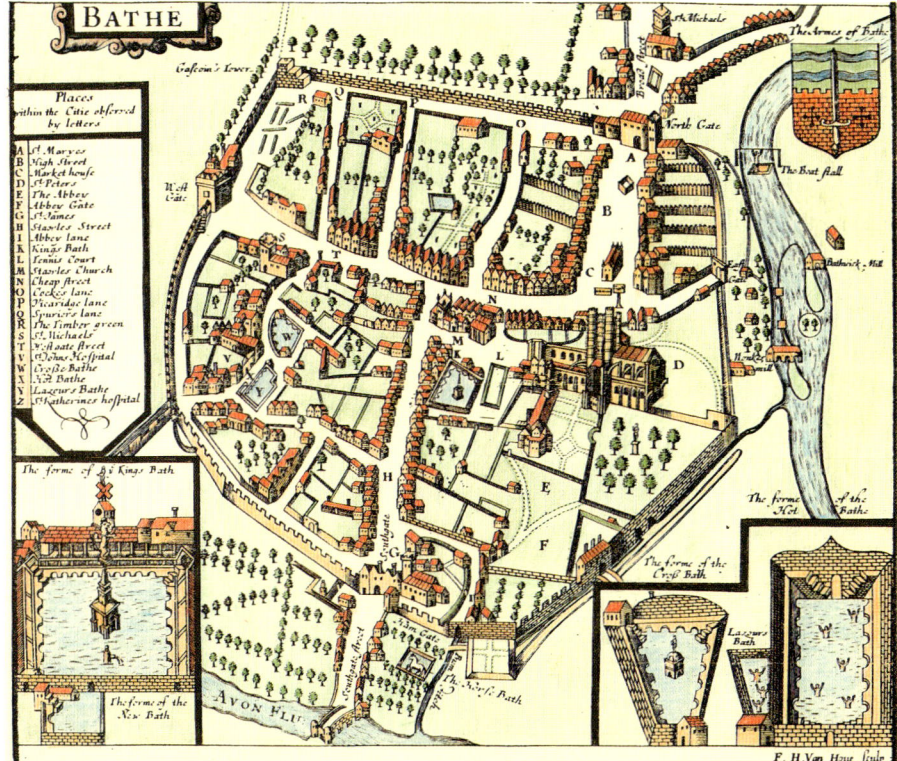

Below: John Speed's map published in 1610 shows the abbey precinct shortly after the Dissolution and before being redeveloped by the City. The nave is represented still without a roof.

Georgian Elegance – Victorian Revival

Under the regime of Beau Nash, the abbey became part of the social round for the frivolous society of that time, and a daily visit for Matins was not unusual. The abbey bells were rung to welcome distinguished visitors – who were afterwards asked to pay for this honour. Contemporary prints show the nave peopled with strolling couples, the ladies with parasols, one with a dog on a lead. During the fashionable 'season' the Sunday services were well attended and many visiting clergymen were invited to preach. The congregation could be very generous in providing substantial sums for charity and the sermons provided topics for subsequent conversation and correspondence.

Although the principal duties of the 'chairmen' were to carry their well-wrapped passengers from the hot baths to their lodgings, they would also be seen in the abbey. It was not unusual for a lady to be brought in a sedan chair and placed in a prominent position for the length of the service. A glance at the memorials on the walls will show the rich variety of people who would be found in the congregation of this period.

The Victorian era brought a more serious consideration of the building. Bath City Corporation was now in charge, so it was at their expense that an extensive restoration was carried out in 1833 under the direction of the City Architect, G. P. Manners.

Pinnacles were added to the turrets of the tower, and hollow flying buttresses erected on each side of the nave. The square turrets on the east front were changed to an octagonal form; the great west doors were repaired and re-carved. Some alterations were also made within the church. Among other changes, the wrought iron communion rail, gift of Field Marshal George Wade in 1725, was sold and replaced.

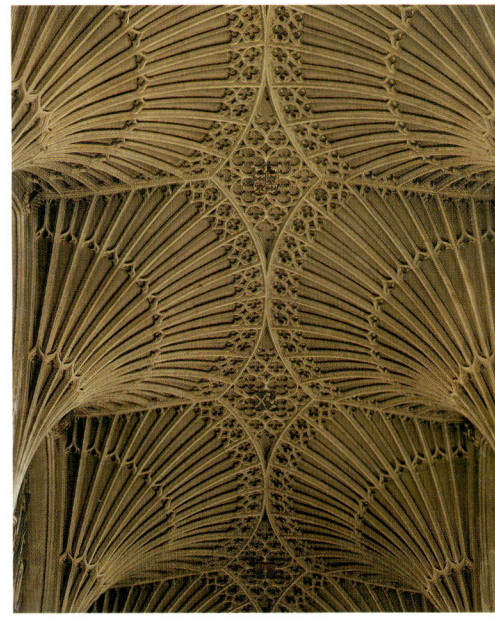

Right:
Perhaps the most outstanding feature of Bath Abbey is the beautiful fan vaulting designed by William Vertue, master mason (or architect as we would say now) to Henry VII.

Below left:
The organ was moved to this position from the nave screen in 1860. The main case was designed by Sir Thomas Jackson in 1914 and the positiv case by Alan Rome in 1972.

Below:
This carved black oak figure of King David originally surmounted the organ on the screen across the nave.

(This iron rail was bought by William Beckford and used as a balcony at his house in Lansdown Place West. Lady Noble, recognizing the decorative rail, returned it to the abbey, where it was converted for use as a screen beneath the organ loft in 1959.)

Perhaps the most important change at this time was the removal of the houses close to, or attached to the north (High Street) side of the abbey. Building here had gradually developed since the 1550s and in spite of the efforts of Marshal Wade ('Wade's Passage') it was not until 1834 that the last of these houses was removed.

The most important influence on the interior of the church since the Vertue brothers conceived their original design was the result of the appointment of a wealthy, far-seeing and competent administrator, Charles Kemble, as Rector in 1859.

He called in Sir George Gilbert Scott as architectural adviser and together the two men devised a scheme of alterations and improvement that would be unthinkable today.

The Bishop Montagu ceiling of lath and plaster was removed and a new stone vaulting built to match the original fan vaulting in the choir. The tall screen which separated the choir from the nave (and which also supported the organ) was taken down and used for some years as a porch at the west end. The organ was moved into the north transept where one can still see the carved wooden figure of King David which, with similar carvings of St Peter and St Paul, adorned the topmost part of the screen, above the organ.

The removal of the screen opened up the vista enjoyed today and, with the levelling of the floor and provision of the oak pews, the church became very much as we see it now. The stone reredos was also designed and installed by Scott, and during this long period of vigorous reorganization of the interior, memorial monuments on the stone pillars were moved to the walls, and the completion of many of the Victorian stained glass windows was achieved. Before his death in 1874, Prebendary Kemble would have seen most of these major works completed. He and his family contributed over £40,000 to the cost, but many other benefactors gave generously to enable other church furnishings to be installed during this time, such as the lectern, communion rail, pulpit, font, altar and chandeliers. Throughout this period of reorganization, although the building work took priority on weekdays, no service was omitted on a Sunday.

Meanwhile some alterations and restoration work affected the appearance of the exterior of the church, and the provision of pinnacles on the turrets caused such an outcry that the local newspaper described it as 'the pinnacle war'. The ones that we see now are those designed by Sir George Gilbert Scott, after two previous styles had been thought unsatisfactory.

Above:
Walking in the centre of Bath we are frequently reminded of the presence of the great church, as seen in this view from the south west, below the archway in York Street. From here we can admire the proportions of the building, the tower, flying buttresses and the battlemented, pierced parapets.

The Monuments

There are over 600 memorial wall tablets in Bath Abbey – more than any other English church apart from Westminster Abbey – and they provide a fascinating and rich social history of 400 years. The style of writing has changed very considerably in this time; as the Revd J. J. Conybeare wrote in 1824, 'The rhetorical epitaph became very popular after the Restoration, and was in some instances extended to a most fatiguing length'.

Dr Samuel Johnson (1709–84) made the famous remark: 'In lapidary inscriptions, a man is not upon oath'. Here is a brief selection from a resource that will repay much further attention.

Dr Henry Harington, musician and author, was Mayor of Bath in 1793. He published many musical works and is reputed to be the author of the much quoted epigram:
These walls so full of monument and bust
Show how Bath waters serve to lay the dust'.

His own memorial is in the north choir aisle.

Below:
Bishop Montagu
The largest monument in the abbey is in memory of James Montagu, Bishop of Bath and Wells 1608–15 and Bishop of Winchester 1615–18. Commissioned by Sir Charles Montagu, it was designed by William Cuer and carved by Nicholas Johnson.

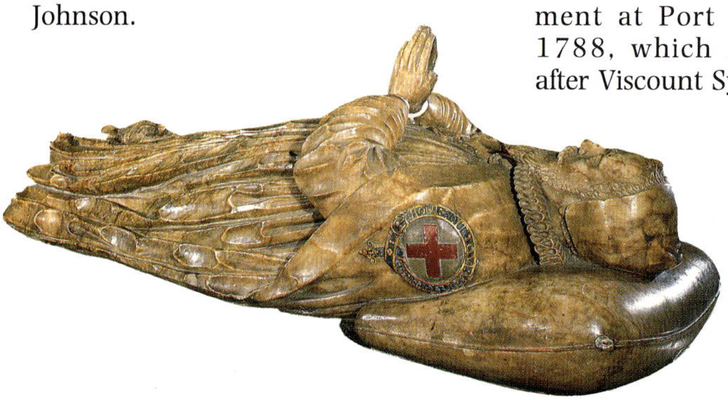

Right:
Lady Waller
Below the Jesse window in the south transept stands the alabaster tomb by Epiphanius Evesham to Jane, wife of Sir William Waller, a Parliamentarian general defeated by Sir Ralph Hopton at the Battle of Lansdown, 1643. The blank space was intended for Sir William's epitaph but he was interred elsewhere.

Above:
Jacob Bosanquet
Scenes such as the Good Samaritan replaced historic bas-reliefs during the 18th century. The earliest of this type in the abbey is dedicated to Jacob Bosanquet, who died in 1767. It is an exquisite fine relief by W. Carter.

Right:
Admiral Phillip
Admiral Arthur Phillip (1738–1814) was founder and first governor of New South Wales. He established the first settlement at Port Jackson in 1788, which he named after Viscount Sydney.

Left:
Richard (Beau) Nash (18)
A plain tablet to the memory of Richard (Beau) Nash, Master of Ceremonies at Bath during the first half of the 18th century. The outstanding social functionary of his day, he made the city a 'Temple of Fashion'. Benevolent at heart, he made every effort to bring into being the Royal Mineral Water Hospital, now important as a centre for the treatment of rheumatic disease.

The Reeve Family (19)
To the left of the memorial to William Bingham, there is a modest brass plaque engraved with the moving story of the Reeve family. The simple verse is decorated by the representation of a cleft skull and a winged hour-glass.

Neare to this place lyeth the body of mary late wife of george Reeve goldfmith of this citty (and alfo of spencer his father and of katherine his mother) and of spencer his firft sonne and of george his fecond sonne and of henry his third sonne and of spencer his fourth sonne.

> *So that you see gaynft deaths alconquering hand*
> *Nor sex nor age agaynft his force can stand*
> *But ther's a tyme wherin our body's muft*
> *Revive agayne though now turn'd into duft:*
>
> *shee departed this life iuly 7th 1664*

Left:
Hon. William Bingham (19)
This senator of the USA founded the first bank in that country (Bank of North America) and he is said to have been a friend of George Washington. He died in 1804 aged 49. The marble carving is by Flaxman.

Above:
William Hoare RA. (12)
A memorial by Chantrey to William Hoare, RA, a portrait painter and contemporary of Gainsborough, who died in 1792.

Above:
Bartholomew Barnes (10)
One of the earliest memorials (1608), this fine marble shows the husband and wife kneeling at a prie-dieu: below the former, his son and a swathed infant; and below the wife, five daughters in the attitude of prayer. The period costume is shown in fine detail.

Bells, Books and Candlesticks

The Organ
The north transept contains a magnificent organ, rebuilt in 1972 by Hill, Norman & Beard. It is the last of a long series of instruments going back at least as far as the 17th century, when Samuel Pepys wrote in his diary, 'Here is a good organ'. There are 4,242 speaking pipes; the main case was designed by Sir Thomas Jackson in 1914 and the positiv case by Alan Rome in 1972.

The Bells
The central tower rises 162 feet, and contains a ringing chamber and a peal of ten bells. The first was bought at Keynsham in the time of Queen Elizabeth I, five others being added soon after at a cost of £206. These were recast into a peal of eight in 1700 and two more were given in 1774. Each carries an inscription, such as 'When you me ring I sweetly sing', 'God prosper the Church of England': and on the 58 inch Tenor Bell 'All you of Bathe that heare me sound Thank Lady Hopton's hundred pound, Abra.Rudhall cast us all Ano.Do.1774'.

The Choir Vestry
Attached to the south side of the nave is a covered cloister, now the choir vestry, designed in 1923 by Sir Thomas Jackson as a memorial to all who fell in the First World War 1914–18. On the outer wall of the nave and within the cloister a number of fragments from the Saxon abbey and Norman cathedral are displayed. One of the earliest relics is the arm of an 8th-century Wessex cross, known as St Aldhelm's cross, found in the vicinity of the Cross Bath.

In 1867, two 12th-century capitals from the Norman cathedral were found inserted in the wall of a mill at Batheaston. Probably from the west front, they date from the episcopate of Robert, Bishop of Bath, who rebuilt the church after the fire of 1137. One depicts St Lawrence undergoing martyrdom on a gridiron. The other shows the flaying of St Bartholomew.

Prior appointment must be made to view this area.

The Library
During the episcopacy of Bishop Lake, the successor of Bishop Montagu, a library was founded in 1619 and housed in the vestry. This collection contains many literary treasures including Voragine's *The Golden Legend* (1493), from the press of Caxton's successor, Wynkyn de Worde. Among the donors appear such names as Bishops Creighton and Ken, Sir William Waller and Joseph Glanvill, Rector of Bath Abbey, 1666–80. The books were moved to Wells in 1983 and are now housed in the cathedral library there.

The Silver
The altar cross and candlesticks were designed by Leslie Durbin and dedicated in 1963.

Unfortunately at present, no safe facility exists to display the abbey collection of antique silver.

Above: ①
The west door was given by Lord Chief Justice Sir Henry Montagu in 1617.

Left: ⑰
The lectern, in the form of an eagle, the sign of St John the Evangelist.

Left: ⑥
Book of Remembrance. This is beautifully illuminated by Benjamin Maslen and contains the names of over 400 civilians and service personnel killed in Bath during the bombing in April 1942.

Right:
During west front conservation work in 1992, the only statue to be replaced was St Philip, by Laurence Tindall of Nimbus Carving.

The Future

Bath Abbey looks back over more than 1,300 years of existence as a site for Christian worship and life. Its history is in many ways the history of Bath itself: first the pagan Britons coming out of the forest to gaze with superstitious awe at the hot springs; then the Romans developing the baths and uniting the local cult with the worship of Minerva, to be supplanted in turn by the dynamic message of the Christian faith. The growing importance of the church as monastic centre and episcopal seat led to its association with our monarchy, through the coronation of King Edgar; the impatient intervention of Queen Elizabeth I, on down to the celebration of 1,000 years of monarchy in 1973 attended by our present royal family.

The Christian faith, however, always calls us to face the challenges and the needs of the future. Now we are approaching the quincentenary in 1999 of our present church, and the fresh demands which the 21st century of the Christian era will lay upon us. We are already looking ahead at ways in which we can present the faith more effectively. May Bath Abbey long continue to shine as 'the Lantern of the West'.

Right and Below:
This guidebook has endeavoured to trace the history of the abbey down through the centuries. It is right that we should remind ourselves finally that the building exists to house the living Church of today and tomorrow. Our two photographs illustrate that Church, in the one picture gathered for Sunday worship, in the other, going out into the abbey churchyard for a special Easter act of witness. An average Sunday will see some 700 people attending our six services, while the big festivals more than double that congregation. Christian worship here for over 1,300 years is a living tradition that feeds the Christian faith into the life of our city and beyond.

A Prayer

O Lord Jesus Christ,
the light of the minds that know you,
the life of the souls that love you,
help us —
so to know you that we may better love you,
so to love you that we may fully serve you,
whom to serve is perfect freedom.

Amen